super

RUGBY

Clive Gifford

Illustrated by Tony Kerins
Consultant: Wayne Wedgbury

Hodder
Children's
Books

a division of Hodder Headline

To Bob for his great enthusiasm for rugby union, rugby league and Australian rules football and to Thea for putting up with Bob's enthusiasm!

Text copyright 1998 © Clive Gifford
Illustrations copyright 1998 © Tony Kerins
Published by Hodder Children's Books 1999

Edited by Anna Davidson
Designed by Fiona Webb
Series designed by Fiona Webb

10 9 8 7 6 5 4 3 2 1

A catalogue record for this book is available from the British Library.

ISBN: 0340 79165 9

Printed by Clays Ltd, St Ives plc

Hodder Children's Books
a division of Hodder Headline
338 Euston Road
London NW1 3BH

Meet the author

Clive Gifford is a widely respected author with more than a dozen sports and leisure books in print, from juggling to football.

A keen sportsman, Clive represented his university at a number of sports, but not rugby – his glass-bottle specs made that quite impossible. At school, though, he built quite a reputation as a go-getting full-back with a good place-kicking boot and an unerring ability to finish a game with a cleaner shirt than any other player on his team. Clive's specs made it impossible for him to progress further in rugby, but that hasn't stopped him from continuing to follow the game in all its forms, especially his favourite teams: in rugby league, the Salford Reds and Brisbane Broncos; in union, Sale; in rugby sevens, Fiji. Clive even had a game of touch-sevens with several Fijian internationals although their idea of "touch" was a shock to Clive who took a couple of years to recover!

A keen rugby fan, Clive has watched and commentated on games as far afield as Brisbane, Bath and Bahia de Caraquez (in Ecuador, South America – he had to check, too.)

Clive would like to thank the first 15 that made this book possible. The top class pack comprised of Keef, Cath, Martin, Dave, Andy, Liz, Gita and Mary. The half backs were Anna Davidson and Anne Clark – they pulled all the strings. And not forgetting the centres and wings, Andra, Kerry, Tony and Jane. Finally, a big thank you to full-back Ian Batty, who place-kicked stray ideas firmly into touch.

Introduction

Whether you're pulling on your shirt and psyching yourself up for a school game or sitting down in front of the telly for an absorbing international match, you know that rugby is as good as team sport gets. Watching or taking part in last-ditch defence, a powerful forward drive or a pulsating attacking move are incredibly exciting thrills to experience.

Rugby requires highly developed individual and team skills. It's a sport that's long on physical commitment and short on prima donnas. If you aren't up for a few bumps and bruises, stick to chess or croquet. But if you're into being fit and playing sports with others, and several million men and women, boys and girls, across more than a hundred countries reckon they are, then it may just be the most rewarding sport you can take up.

Clive

Contents

Introducing rugby

All kinds of rugby

Rugby comes in many different flavours, from rugby sevens to mini rugby, but what we're concentrating on in this book is the 15-a-side game of rugby union. (Rugby league, a different code, but one which shares a number of the same skills is looked at in the very last chapter.) Full rugby union is what you are most likely to watch on television with such highlights as the Five Nations, the Tri-Nations and the World Cup. Many of you may play mini rugby. Some of you may play touch, tag or new image rugby at school. All of these games are designed to develop basic skills so that, as you get older, you can make the steps up to the full game with ease. We've looked long and hard at these basic skills and how they work in the full game and, in places where the rules are quite different, we've explained those differences. In doing this, we think we have provided an exciting and useful guide to both playing and watching rugby – the ultimate team game.

Whatever version of the game you currently play, rugby requires commitment, passion and skill from all players on the field. Players must constantly work hard for each other. But, enough of telling you why rugby is so good and on to making you good at rugby!

Let's start with the basic object of the game: getting the oval-shaped ball behind the opponent's try line and placed down on the turf. This is a try, which nets your team points, followed by a further point or points scored by kicking the ball between the goal posts for a conversion.

The ball is moved up the field towards the try line by team members passing to the side or back (never forwards). The only ways a player can make the ball travel forwards is by kicking it or running forwards with it in hand.

Introducing rugby

The team without the ball defends their try line and looks
to get the ball back in their possession. There are a number
of set plays, such as scrummages, for when play has broken
down or the ball has gone out of bounds. Sometimes, one
team or the other does something wrong, such as being
offside or fouling the opposition. This usually results in
some form of penalty, such as the ball being given to the
opposition or a penalty kick for points being awarded.
The referee's word is taken as final in rugby and should
never be contested.

*Teams defend as a unit, spreading across the field to stop the
opposition breaking through and tackling the player with the ball to
try to win possession.*

Mini rugby

There's every chance that you play mini rugby. It's a brilliant development – a cut down version of the full game of rugby union intended to give every player on the field a chance at building and honing his or her basic rugby skills. In mini rugby, there is less reliance on set pieces and brute power and far more emphasis on handling, passing, moving and tackling skills. These skills are vital in the full game and what you learn in mini rugby will serve you well in the future. Mini rugby's rules change slightly according to age. Each age group learns new skills and the rules adjust accordingly, as players get older and more skilled.

Backs in the team not awarded the scrummage must stand at least 7m back from the scrummage.

Scrums are uncontested.

Scrum-half stands 1m away from scrummage.

In under-9 and under-10 mini rugby, the teams form three-man scrummages.

Introducing rugby

Mini rugby is usually played across a full-size rugby pitch.
The recommended overall dimensions for under 9s and 10s
is 59m x 35m and for under 11s and under 12s, 59m x 43m.
The pitch we show here is that used for the under 10s and
9s. A full-size pitch is shown on pages 20–21. The duration
of games varies according to age. These are shown on
page 22.

In the under 9s and under 10s, as shown below there are
nine players a side, divided into three forwards and six backs.
In the under 11s and 12s game, 12 players form a team with
five forwards and seven backs.

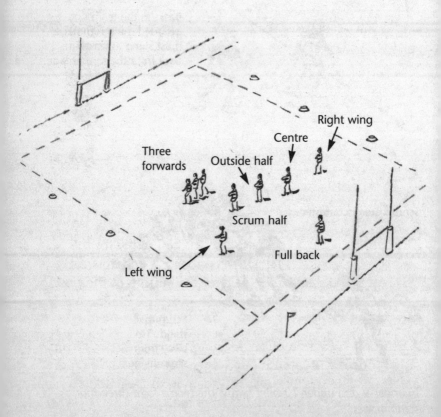

Free passes

Mini rugby makes a lot of use of free passes for when there are infringements such as obstruction, offside, kicking the ball or feeding the ball in a scrummage. The offending team must retreat 7m from where the free pass is to be made. Free passes are also used in the under 10s and under 9s version to start each half of the game.

Always look to pass with two hands.

A free pass, like all passes in mini rugby must be thrown sideways or backwards.

Conversions

There are no kicks to convert a try in mini rugby for the under 9s and under 10s. For the under 11s and above, conversion kicks are always taken from in front of the posts.

No hand-offs

A hand-off involves a player levering themselves away from an opponent with a push of an open hand, not a swing of an arm or fist. You'll be allowed them in the full, adult game, but they're outlawed in mini rugby.

11

New initiatives

There are a number of new developments in rugby for youngsters. Each country has its own name for their own new approach to rugby for the young and this can all get a little confusing. The good thing is that, although there may be minor rule and technique differences amongst the range, the basic principles are the same.

Touch rugby

Brilliant for practising and developing running and passing skills, touch rugby replaces full contact tackles with a two-handed touch by a "tackler" on the hips of the player with the ball. You can play touch rugby with family and friends safe in the knowledge that no one is going to get injured. It allows you to focus on passing, running and, for the defence, tracking attackers. The great thing with touch rugby is that you can play your own version of it pretty much anywhere. Providing you mark out a pitch and agree the rules beforehand, you can have plenty of fun with five, six or more a side.

Pitch marked by lines in the sand.

Use sand or clothing as markers.

Make sure you play well away from others.

Tag rugby

It can sometimes be hard to judge whether a two-handed touch tackle has been made so tag rugby features an ingenious little device to make tackling more clearcut and the game more fair as well as great fun. Every player wears a tag belt, which has two ribbons attached to it with Velcro. Pulling off one of the ribbons and shouting "tag" counts as a tackle. The player about to be tackled can try to swerve away from the tackle but cannot fend it off or shield the ribbons. Once tackled, the defender steps back one metre and the tackled player must immediately pass the ball. After passing, the defender hands back the ribbon, which the player must reattach before getting back into the game.

New image rugby

A form of organised touch rugby that can be played by girls and boys, dads and mums. Any number from 12-a-side right down to three or four-a-side is possible but make sure that the pitch size reduces as the numbers do! Four points for a try are awarded and typical rugby laws such as no knock-ons or forward passes are allowed. New image rugby features touches on the hips as a tackle and includes simple scrums and line-outs as well. The Rugby Football Union (address on page 124) have further details on the game.

History mystery

Rugby is proud of its history and reveres the great players, sides and matches of yesteryear. It's a bit of a mystery why, when it all started with a schoolboy who cheated. The legend goes that in 1823, during a game of football at a public school, one pupil, William Webb Ellis, caught the ball and then ran with it. As a result, a handling version of football became popular and it was named after Webb Ellis's school. Lucky it was his school, Rugby, rather than mine. The Stanwell and District Secondary Comprehensive would have been an awfully long and dull name for a team sport.

In later life, the cheeky schoolboy grew up to become a Reverend and a pillar of the community.
[See, there's hope for you, yet!]

In truth, despite Webb Ellis's antics, people had often played games using feet to kick a ball and hands to carry or throw it. But once rugby got under way, it spread like wildfire. Everyone wanted to play this fast-moving, exciting game. Too many at times, as 50-a-side or more games occurred in towns and villages which were little more than slightly organised mass brawls.

I can't wait for when the game is scaled down to only 15-a-side!

In 1845, a set of rules was drawn up and over the years these were added to and tinkered with. Clubs started to form, some of which are still around, such as Blackheath (1858), and Richmond and Sale (1863). In 1871, the first-ever rugby international occurred (between England and Scotland). Australia and New Zealand quickly caught on, so much so that when England toured the Pacific in 1888, two New Zealand sides beat them – something English rugby has had to get used to over the years!

The 1890s saw a split in rugby. Some, mainly northern, clubs and players wished to be compensated for time off work. Being paid to play is called professionalism and it was resisted by the gentlemen amateurs running the game of rugby at the time. This led to a breakaway Northern Football Union in 1895, which created rugby league. A century later, the powers that be allowed rugby union to go professional too.

Rugby today: the big competitions

From your local schools cup to the national leagues run for professional or semi-professional teams, more and more rugby matches are being played within the framework of some competition or other. Below are some of the biggest and best known.

The Five, sorry, Six Nations

Stemming from the irregular international matches played between England, Scotland, Wales and Ireland, the Five Nations added France to an annual competition that is always fascinating to watch no matter who wins the trophy. Rivalries are intense as sides aim for the Grand Slam – beating all the other teams. The 2000 competition included Italy as a sixth side for the first time.

Tri-nations and the Super 12 series

Down under, there is a three-way contest between the big guns, South Africa, Australia and New Zealand, and also a demanding competition between the best 12 provinces from Australia, New Zealand and South Africa. The Super 12 provides tough, often exhilarating rugby watched by average crowds of more than 30,000 per game and millions more on T.V.

The World Cup

The Rugby World Cup started in 1987 and is the jewel in the sport's crown. The 1999 competition hosted by Wales with some games played in England, Ireland, Scotland and France saw over 70 national sides attempt to qualify for a tournament won by Australia. France's thrilling win over the New Zealand All Blacks was the game of the tournament watched by millions of people all over the world.

The women's World Cup was first held in 1991 in South Wales and was a huge success. The USA beat England 19–6 in the final. The 1998 competition saw New Zealand hoist the trophy.

Touring teams

Apart from set international competitions, other highlights of the rugby calendar include matches played by touring international sides. The Lions is a touring squad picked from all four home nations – that's England, Wales, Scotland and Ireland – and for a player from these countries, taking part is still the highest honour in the game. The rise of the World Cup initially placed doubts as to whether the British Lions would continue, but an incredible series win against South Africa in 1997 has confirmed that a Lions tour is still a major event.

2 Let's get going

Kitted-out

Good news. You don't need a king's ransom to afford rugby kit. Basically, it's shirts, shorts, socks and boots. Boots are the only item of kit you really need to worry about. Modern rugby boots come in two styles: the high-cut boot with ankle protection and the low-cut boot, similar to that used in football.

When you go to the shops looking to buy a pair of boots, check the boot is flexible and comfortable. Look for comfortable padding around your foot. A shock-absorbing insole can be fitted to add extra comfort and support.

Screw-in studs allow you to vary stud length within the laws (the rugby rules and regulations) for different conditions. Studs must not have sharp edges nor be too long. A single stud at the toe of the boot is also not allowed. Choose standard studs (kite mark BS6366) or boots with a moulded rubber multi-studded sole.

18

No watches, rings, earrings or other items that may stick out and cause an injury are allowed.

Rugby shirts and shorts tend to be made of heavy cotton. Apart from being comfortable, cotton tends to be hard-wearing.

Mouthguards are worn by many players. A mouthguard can feel uncomfortable at first but can save you your teeth and cost far, far less than visits to the dentist.

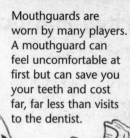

A rugby ball can be made of leather or synthetic material. Balls come in different sizes - Mini (3), Junior (4) and Adult (5).

Keep your shirt tucked in. Apart from looking smarter, it stops it flapping around and providing something for an opponent to grab and catch you with.

Socks should be kept up with ties.

A tracksuit for warming up and warming down is important.

Some players like to wear shin guards to protect their lower legs.

Pitch and positions

The pitch

If you fancy yourself as a great rugby artist, then here is your blank canvas, the full-size rugby pitch, together with some basic player positions for the full 15-a-side game.

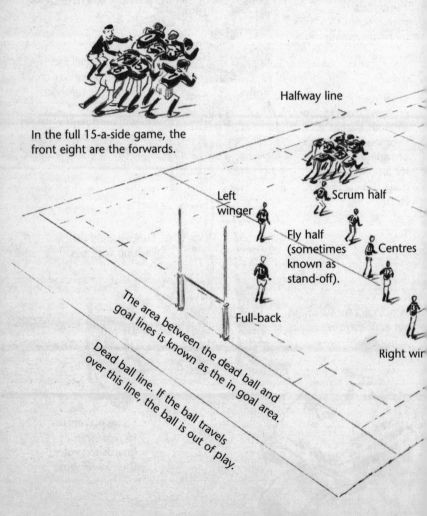

Halfway line

In the full 15-a-side game, the front eight are the forwards.

Left winger

Scrum half

Fly half (sometimes known as stand-off).

Centres

Full-back

Right wir

The area between the dead ball and goal lines is known as the in goal area.

Dead ball line. If the ball travels over this line, the ball is out of play.

Positions and decisions

The full game features an eight-man scrum incorporating all the forwards, numbers one to eight. Numbers nine and ten in a full-size game, the scrum half and stand-off, are the key decision makers in a game. They choose where the ball goes, whether it is kicked, run with, passed back to the forwards or spun out wide in an attacking move to the centres, wings and full-back (known collectively as the backs).

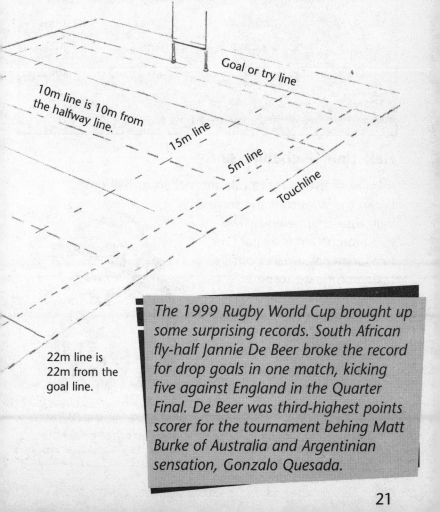

Goal or try line

10m line is 10m from the halfway line.

15m line

5m line

Touchline

22m line is 22m from the goal line.

The 1999 Rugby World Cup brought up some surprising records. South African fly-half Jannie De Beer broke the record for drop goals in one match, kicking five against England in the Quarter Final. De Beer was third-highest points scorer for the tournament behing Matt Burke of Australia and Argentinian sensation, Gonzalo Quesada.

Time, please

Full rugby is played as two halves of 40 minutes with any time for stoppages added to the end of each half. Junior games are also played in halves but are shorter in duration. The small box below gives typical timings for mini rugby matches.

AGE GROUP	TIME PLAYED EACH WAY I.E. PER HALF		
	Single Fixture	Triangular Tournament	Festival
U11/U12	- 20 mins	15 mins	7 mins
U9/U10	- 15 mins	10 mins	7 mins
U7/U8	- 10 mins	7½ mins	5 mins

Festivals are events with lots of teams present. Usually, no more than five games are allowed per team.

Half time – change ends

A break of five or more minutes occurs at half-time. When the sides start the second half, they change ends. The half-time period is a vital time in all matches. Apart from taking on board some liquid, a team can regroup and talk about the half ahead. Listen to your captain and more-experienced players around you. If you have a point, keep it brief and never shout anyone else down. Remember, you're a team and you're all in the game together.

Don't worry about the slope, lads. Sixty-eight nil should be a big enough cushion

Warming up

Before the game, some time should be spent warming up and getting prepared for the match ahead. All players, no matter how fit or skilful, should warm up. This takes the form of plenty of stretching of your leg, back and shoulder muscles. It should also feature some jogging and exercises like star jumps to get the blood circulating, and some drills or handling practice to get the feel of the ball and get your mind in gear for the game ahead. Although you may be worn out after a match, a gentle warm down with a few more stretches can ease your aching muscles and allow you to recover more quickly.

Total rugby

The traditional view

The 15-a-side full game used to call for different players with quite different attributes filling the positions.

Okay, this may be a humorous view but it was the thinking then. Now, the game is all about developing similar skills, so backs have to be good tacklers and capable of rucking and mauling, whilst forwards have to be far more mobile than before and possess decent ball-handling skills. It all adds up to the big buzzwords in the sport today – "total rugby". Total rugby is about skills being almost interchangeable between positions.

Being versatile is especially important for you as you're still growing and filling out. Don't pigeonhole yourself as a one position player. Instead, enjoy where you play now but work hard on developing all your skills and your fitness so that as your physique changes and your playing requirements alter, you will be ready for a different position.

Technique over strength

Your changing body size and shape prompts another vital point. You should be working on technique and developing your rugby brain not pumping iron. Sure, you'll occasionally come up against huge players of your age who are much stronger. Be patient as nature tends to have a way of evening things out. Concentrate on the skills of the game until you're more fully grown. Fitness should be worked on at training sessions and generally by practising sprints and playing and enjoying plenty of sport.

Remember, too, that every person is different. What works for a friend may not work for you. Seek out your coach for advice on a dedicated fitness programme tailored to you.

Does size matter?

Rugby is deliberately designed as a game for all shapes and sizes. Sure, if you're small for your age and are not growing, it's unlikely you'll make it into the Lions second row. But remember, there are plenty of small adult rugby players – Welsh international Arwel Thomas at 1.73m and 70kg is one shining example.

The referee

The referee must know, understand and be able to apply every law whilst covering the pitch as well as any fit winger or flanker. It's just as well that almost every good referee was or still is a rugby player.

The referee has a large number of signals with which he communicates his decisions. Here are some of the most common:

Try

Penalty

Free kick

Advantage

Scrummage (outstretched hand points to side who get put-in)

Respect

Referees are completely respected and their word is final. And so it should be – rugby players know that the ref isn't a spoilsport but is there to make a match as enjoyable and safe as possible for all players. Never mouth off or disagree with an official's decisions. Respect also applies to the opposition players – foul or dangerous play, from high tackles around the neck and head to a bout of fisticuffs, is plain stupid and unnecessary. No one on your team will thank you for giving away a penalty or being sent off.

High tackle

Knock on

Not releasing the ball

Obstructing or crossing

Touch judges

The referee is assisted by two touch judges. These officials run the line during most of the game but stand under the goal posts when a penalty kick or conversion kick between the posts takes place, to check whether the ball went through or not. Here are the touch judges' main signals.

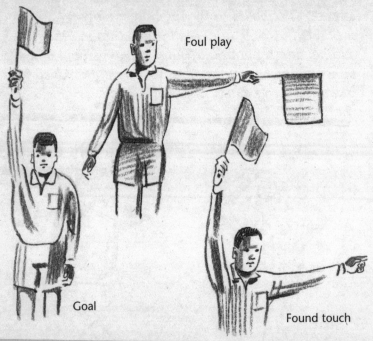

Foul play

Goal

Found touch

The laws of the game

Throughout the book, we've mentioned some key laws, but by no means have we detailed each and every rugby law. It's important that you're aware of them, though, and a copy of the Laws Of The Game is recommended reading. (Turn to page 122 to see how you can obtain a copy of the latest set.) I'm not going to lie to you – rugby's laws are long and complex – but if you want to progress as a player, you must know them.

Obstruction

Obstruction is unfairly getting in the way of one or more members of the opposing team. It takes many forms – two classics are tackling or pulling the shirt of a player without the ball and running in front of your team-mate with the ball so blocking off access for tacklers from the opposing team. Don't do it.

The kicker wants to chase the ball but the opposition player has deliberately stepped into his path, obstructing him.

Offside

The world's greatest minds have put a man on the moon and sent robots to Mars, but no genius has yet come up with a short, understandable, complete summary of rugby's involved offside rule!

The idea of penalising offside is good and simple – to give a team space to play the ball when it has won it fairly. On the next two pages are some of the most common offside situations you can find yourself in and what you can and cannot do about it.

OPEN PLAY AND IN FRONT OF THE BALL

In open play, you are offside when you are standing in front of a team-mate who last played the ball or who currently has it. In this situation you can move just as long as you don't obstruct an opponent, play the ball or obtain any form of advantage for your team.

There is no penalty for this sort of offside situation providing you don't do any of the above things, but your team is effectively a man down. You are useless until you get back onside.

These three players are offside.

Player receiving the ball is onside.

OPEN PLAY AND BEHIND THE BALL

When a team-mate who is behind you kicks the ball ahead, you are offside and must not move towards the ball no matter how far ahead it has gone. Stand still or move backwards, taking care not to obstruct an opponent. If you're less than 10m away from an opponent who's looking to field the kick, get out of there and fast! Even if you stand still, you are infringing and the referee could penalise you. Getting 10m away won't stop you from being offside, but it may stop the referee awarding a penalty kick against you.

Players here are
now offside.

GETTING ONSIDE

Once offside, your priority is to get onside so that you're
back in the game. You can run back and behind the ball
carrier or you can let the ball-carrier run, or kick and run,
ahead of you. Another team-mate who was onside can run
ahead of you – all of these situations put you back onside.

There are three other ways you can get onside and these
depend on the opposition. If an opposing player carries
the ball 5m forward, kicks or passes the ball or handles it
intentionally, then you are back onside, providing you
weren't within 10m of him or her.

Old habits...

*All-Black legend, George Nepia, was taking part in a
charity match when the ball came straight to him after
a clearance. Ever alert, he picked it up, spotted a
defensive gap under the posts and scored a try.
Only one problem – he was refereeing the game!*

31

3 Ball handling

The super three skills

You may have heard of the Super 12 – it's the big southern hemisphere competition between the big regional and club sides of rugby powerhouses like Australia, New Zealand and South Africa – but what of the super three? The super three is simply the most important set of skills you must learn to become a decent player:

- Passing and catching
- Tackling
- Running with and without the ball

It doesn't matter whether you're a bull of a prop forward or a willowy full-back – EVERY player must be really good at these three skills. These are so important that we're going to take time to look at them over the next couple of chapters because, without them, being good in the scrum or having a good kicking foot is irrelevant. If you and your team-mates cannot pass, run and tackle, the game's as good as over.

A small advantage
You don't have to be the size of the biggest school bully to succeed at junior rugby. Many of the so-called "big boys" have not developed their game, relying instead on their current strength advantage as a substitute for thinking about or improving their game.

Basic ball skills

Let me start by introducing you to your new best friend, the rugby ball. If you have it in your hands, then your side may be able to score. Certainly, while the ball's in your hands, the opposition cannot. Possession is absolutely vital and possession stems from good ball handling skills.

It doesn't matter whether you're a forward or back, you need excellent ball handling skills to progress. Try to keep a ball with you whenever you can. Throw it up and down, catch it firmly, and with arms shoulder-width apart, move it from one hand to another. This all helps you to build up a feel for the ball.

Use two hands to throw the ball over one shoulder and twist at your waist to catch it cleanly. Watch the flight of the ball all the way into your hands.

Handling the ball

You need to be able to catch before you can pass the ball and building up a feel for a ball is as much about improving catching as it is about learning how to pass. Now before you say something along the lines of, "Doh! We know how to catch, stupid!" let me make one point. Of course, you have a good idea of how to catch a ball at a nice height in front of you that arrives just when you expect it. But in a match, rarely does the ball arrive on a silver platter in this way. A combination of oval ball shape, wind, wet and greasy conditions along with the rigours of the actual game means that the ball will come your way from all sorts of unexpected directions and angles and at varying speeds. Catching in these situations is hard, which is why you want to build and improve your reactions. Over the next few pages, there are plenty of individual and group practices that will help and can also be incorporated in pre-match warm up exercises. You can even invent your own variations.

High ball

Throw the ball up high and straight so that you have to move your feet as little as possible to get under the ball to catch it at chest height.

Drop ball

Release the ball at head height and get your hands down quickly to catch it before it reaches the floor.

Under your leg

Stand with your feet shoulder-width apart. Lift one leg, bending it at the knee. Pass the ball from one hand to the other around the outside of your thigh and under the leg you have lifted. Lower that leg, raise your other leg and repeat by passing the ball around the other leg. Work on getting this down to a smooth flowing action.

Catching tips

For all types of catches, remember these top tips:

- Create a target area with your hands for the passer to aim a pass at.
- Watch the ball into your hands as long as possible.
- Spread your fingers and catch with your fingers to get a good grasp of the ball.
- As the ball comes into your hands, draw your hands in and down to cushion the ball's landing.
- Get the ball in both hands firmly under control.

The lateral pass

Right, on to the basic pass, the one you will use throughout a game. It's called the lateral pass, which means a pass sideways. Two hands are used throughout the pass. The ball is held in the hands lengthways with your fingers pointing along the ball's seams. The ball should be held only in the fingers.

Carry the ball at chest height and check your target – your receiver – just before you make the pass. Swing your arms across your body towards the receiver.

Push the ball with your rear hand (your right, if you're making a pass to the left). You guide the ball's direction with your other hand. Flick your wrists and fingers as the ball leaves your hands.

Watch the ball as it travels away from you. You must follow through as you do in a football kick or a golf swing. Make sure your fingers point to your target.

Passing standing still

Stand three or more players in a line so that only your fingertips can touch. Now, from one end of the line to the other, pass the ball while standing still. Use your waist to rotate and stretch your arms out to keep both hands on the ball as you hand it on to the next player. Once you've passed the ball, face the other way. Pass it back and forth down the line. The ball should never actually be thrown – there should always be one or two pairs of hands on it.

Easy, eh? Well, now take two large paces away from each other and repeat the move – except now you're passing the ball properly.

Both hands on ball.

Select target area – the outstretched hands of the player you're passing to.

Switch players around in the middle regularly.

Twist at waist to sweep the ball across you and release pass.
Receiving player focuses on ball reaching hands.

Pass strength and direction

The long and short of it

The basic lateral pass is incredibly versatile; it can be used to pass either to the left or right and works for distances from a couple of metres to 10m or more. For short passes, little force is required. For long passes, more effort is needed. Only you can get used to the amount of force required to send the ball different distances. This is why you must practise as much as you can.

For a very short pass, often called a pop pass, hold the ball at chest height and flick your fingers and wrists gently to send the ball up and towards the receiver.

For a longer pass than usual, you want to swing your shoulders and twist at your waist to add power. Concentrate on controlling the ball's direction.

Both sides please

Many new and intermediate players find it easier to pass to one side than the other. You must be able to pass to both sides so work hard on your weaker side.

Billy-no-mates?

On your own? Well, you can still work a little on pass strength with just a ball and a wall for company. Chalk up a half-metre target circle on the wall and stand at varying distances (between three and twelve paces from the wall). Get used to how much force you need to put into your swing and the flick of your wrists and fingers to get the ball travelling in a low arc to hit the target.

Three-player passing

An excellent passing drill for three players, the middle player starts several paces behind the line created by the other two players. As he walks up into the line, the player with the ball passes. The middle player passes on to the final player, making sure each time that no forward passes are made. The middle player walks ahead, turns around and comes back into the line to repeat the passing sequence but in reverse. Make sure you all take equal turns as the player in the middle.

Passing on the move

Now, let's inject some movement into your passing. Not too fast at first – start with walking and then trotting through all the exercises below. It's vital that you get the basics right before increasing the pace.

If you're on your own, adapt the Billy-no-mates wall exercise on the previous page. Start five paces behind the target, trotting forwards and timing your pass so that it travels sideways or a little behind and hits the target circle. Adjust distances away from the wall and try varying your forward speed before you make the pass.

This is good practice for timing the release and making sure the ball doesn't travel forwards. But it's only you moving. In a real game, there's also the movement of your target receiver to allow for. So grab a mate and pass in pairs.

As you pass the ball between each other, making sure you always pass to the side or back, never forwards, you'll quickly notice how much harder this is than static passing. Your brain is having to work much harder now as it has to calculate where to pass the ball so that it arrives in the correct place. You have to aim slightly ahead of the receiver and it's up to you to judge his speed and the speed and angle of your pass so that by the time the pass gets across to him, it isn't behind him or too far ahead of him to be caught. There's no secret solution to this other than practice and building up experience.

Line passing

Three or four of you can work down the pitch passing the ball in the same way as with pairs but up and down the line. This sort of passing practice is good for warming up and getting a feel of the ball before a training session or an actual match. Build up speed as all of you become more confident of your passing and receiving skills.

Passer ahead of receiver

41

Pass class

There are lots of potential passing drills. Below are just a couple of simple ones to start you off. Follow your coach's drills and even try to think up your own. Remember, a drill should be taken seriously with full concentration and commitment, otherwise it's a waste of time for those taking part.

Passing past defenders

In this versatile drill, you start off with two passers and one defender operating in a 10m wide channel. Walk and then jog through, passing the ball to get past the defender. The defender cannot tackle either player but can attempt to intercept the ball. Passers must make legitimate passes, i.e. not forwards, and work their way along the channel making passes. As you get more confident and proficient, build up the numbers, first to three versus two and finally, three versus three. If the ball is intercepted, dropped or travels outside the channel, then two defenders switch places with the passer and intended receiver.

Passing tips for matches

Timing. It's everything – you must time your pass.

Receiver awareness. Know where your receiver is, where they're heading and learn to judge their speed so you can provide a quality pass.

You're in control. Only make a pass to a player in a better position than you.

You can see what those three things spell, can't you?

Changing directions game

In a 20m square box play three players with the ball to two defenders. Defenders cannot tackle or contact players but must try to block passes and intercept the ball. Attackers are allowed to run and pass in any direction, provided that the ball is passed behind or to the side of whatever direction they are facing. Although not like a real game, where only one direction is forward, this is a fast, fun game that can help sharpen your decision-making and passing skills.

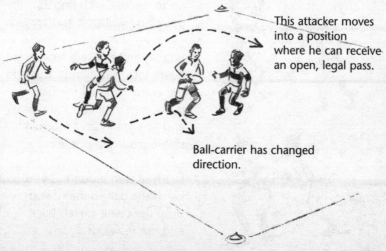

This attacker moves into a position where he can receive an open, legal pass.

Ball-carrier has changed direction.

More ball handling skills

There's plenty more on classy passing moves including dummy, switch and loop passes coming up in other chapters. Here, we'll take a brief look at a couple of important techniques: catching the high ball, spinning a long pass and making a pass off the ground. Before you think of jumping ahead, remember that for every fancy pass you'll make in a game, you'll probably make 10 or more regular lateral passes.

You take the high ball

Catching a high kick is an important skill you should master. First of all, make it clear to team-mates that it's your ball by giving a clear, loud call. Follow the ball's path and estimate where the ball is going to land and get under that point as quickly as possible. Keep your eye on the ball and don't get distracted by the thunderous sound of the hooves of charging opposition players.

Wide stance for balance, side on to opposition. Raise arms with relaxed hands, reaching up to the ball with fingers pointing towards it and spread.

Watch the ball like a hawk right down into your hands. Cushion the catch and pull the ball down into your chest and arms and sink your hips to form a stable crouched position.

Learn to turn around as you catch the ball so that if you drop the ball it travels back and not forwards.

A mark

If you are inside your own 22m area and make a clean catch, you can call a "mark". The referee then orders the opposition to retreat 10m from the kick and your team have to stay behind you. You now have a free kick which can be a tap, place or drop kick (see page 100). Some players prefer to tap kick and then pass to a better kicker, but there's nothing to stop you from looking to find touch with a good kick yourself.

Spin it!

For speedy passes over long distances, you can adapt the lateral pass and spin the ball to use its shape so that it bullets through the air. This is something of an acquired skill so don't be disappointed if you don't manage it overnight or over a month. I know two adult players (who shall remain nameless) who've never got to grips with the spin pass.

One common way to spin the ball is for your rear pushing hand to come up the side and over the top of the ball. You need to snap your wrists and fingers hard to get a good amount of spin on the ball.

Passing off the ground

Depends on the length of pass required; you can use the pop pass shown on page 38 for a short flick on to a nearby team-mate or a swing of the shoulders for a longer pass. The key thing with a pass off the ground is to give yourself a wide stance, both for balance and to make it easier to bend your knees and pick up the ball.

Your weight starts on the leg nearest the ball, but as your arms sweep across your body, your weight is transferred to the other leg.

Look to aim the ball up into your receiver's chest area but no higher.

Follow through with fingers pointing towards the target.

The leading leg is facing the direction of the pass.

Fielding the loose ball

Rugby's inventors in their infinite wisdom have lumbered players with an oval ball, which is fine for passing and kicking but when it hits the turf, chaos can occur.

Getting low while keeping your balance is the key. Keep your eye on the ball as you approach it. Bend from your hips so you are low to the ground and get both hands on the ball. Try to get your feet either side of the ball by the time you are scooping it up. With the ball under your control, you can drive away off your back foot.

Kick or throw the ball so that it lands 5m or so in front of a friend. He must collect it cleanly and then send it back in the same way. If you're on your own you can simply kick the ball ahead 15-20m and chase down your kick. Collect the ball as smoothly as you can and repeat until worn out!

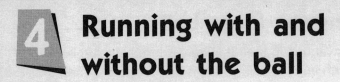

4 Running with and without the ball

Running with the ball

I really should be taking you through all the important material about support play and team passing first, but I know you want to learn about how to beat an opponent in a one-on-one situation. Of course you do, it's one of the most satisfying and exciting moments in a rugby player's life to beat an opponent by pace or trickery.

One-on-one situations can occur when:

1 a successful attacking move leaves the ball carrier with one last defender to beat to score a try.

2 a player launches an attempt to break through the opposition's defence, especially if it is spread thinly.

3 a player receives the ball and moves forwards, but is isolated from team-mates. In this situation, the player can slow up to look for a team-mate to arrive or can try to get past the next line of defence.

Right, so how do you do it? Read on.

Pin back your ears...

Out-and-out speed often is the key, especially if, after a series of phases of play, you are a speedy player and are faced by a heavier, slower player in defence.

Changes of pace

As you'll learn in the next chapter, tacklers have to estimate where you'll be by the time they make contact. Slowing down can make a tackler hesitate as he re-adjusts his tackling position. As he's adjusting, press the accelerator and sprint hard. If you can combine this increased pace with a small swerve or change of running line, the chances of evading a tackle increase.

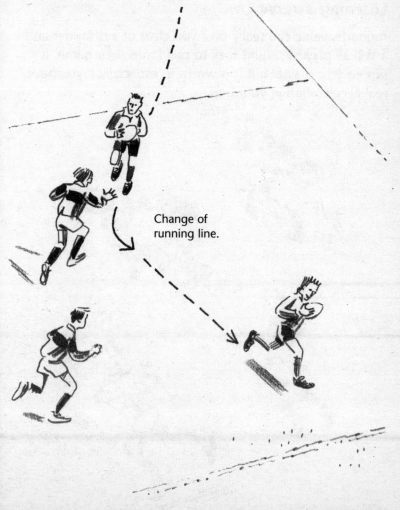

Change of running line.

Evasion

All evasion moves and skills rely on you approaching the defender with your running under control and your body balanced. In effect, sidesteps, swerves and dummy passes are bluffs – you threaten to move or do one thing when in fact you do something else. With that in mind, the fake part of the move must be fully convincing.

Learning swerve

A good swerve can really take you clear of a defender and is a skill all players should seek to build into their game. It's not easy to master but it is worth it, especially if you have real acceleration in your legs.

Approach the defender straight on. Control your running so that you're heading towards the defender's inside shoulder. Keep the ball held into ribs or in both hands.

About four paces short of the defender, swing away with a long stride across the body of the defender. Watch the defender and use the edges of your feet to lean away and swerve around him. Once clear, really step on the gas and accelerate away from him as fast as you can.

Swerve slalom

Practise swerves in one-on-one situations with a team-mate. You do need to swerve to both sides so a slalom made of tackle bags, or better still, a row of players, can be very useful. Run with speed, but always under control, and stay as close as you can to the players without touching them. Always keep the ball to the side furthest from the player you are swerving round.

Row of players three paces apart.

Switch ball so it is always on your side furthest from the tackler.

Lean into tackler using edges of boots for extra grip before swerving around him.

Get to end of row and return back down the slalom, before next player's turn.

Sidesteps and support

Sidestep

Changes of direction can be as devastating as changes in pace. If you're running at an angle to a defender, you can step hard on one foot and push sharply away to change the direction you head in. This is called a sidestep.

Choose the running line you wish to head in and then run away from it to some extent. Plant the foot furthest away from the line of running you intend and shift your body weight to that foot. At this point, the defender is convinced you're going to head in that direction.

Explode off that foot, getting your body weight on your other foot and drive past the defender, watching him constantly. Accelerate into the space to the side of the defender.

Evasion top tips

- Perform sidesteps when running at an angle away from the defender.
- Leave plenty of space between you and the defender with all these moves.
- Don't run so fast that you cannot change direction.

Support

Evasion skills and hard running can work on their own for a while, but if the player with the ball doesn't receive support quickly, then he will be tackled and more than likely, the opposition team will gain possession.

Never let your team's ball-carrier get isolated. There should always be players running with him, offering support. When you see a faster team-mate than you streak off with the ball in hand, don't relax and think, "I can't keep up with him." Run your hardest. Sure, you may be a few metres behind him, but your hard running can often be of great value in giving him a passing option or support if he is tackled.

If you are big for your age...

Make the most of your advantage but don't stop working hard or learning more and more about the game. Why? Well, you may find short-term success just by using your physique but, quicker than you can say "teenager", you'll come up against players who've grown AND have worked hard on aspects of their game. Don't get lazy, get working!

Going around a defence

There are three ways to beat a defence – kick over it, go through it or go around it. Going around a defence is often achieved by having an overlap that is exploited by hard running, support and passing.

Two against one

When you have the ball and a team-mate in support and you are confronted by one defender, you should be as positive as possible. Two against one should equal success for your side. The ball-carrier should try to commit the defender to tackle. This is achieved by running hard at the defender towards his inside shoulder. Once a defender is committed to tackling you, a well-timed pass can release the receiver.

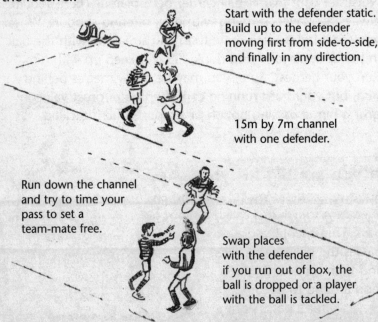

Start with the defender static. Build up to the defender moving first from side-to-side, and finally in any direction.

15m by 7m channel with one defender.

Run down the channel and try to time your pass to set a team-mate free.

Swap places with the defender if you run out of box, the ball is dropped or a player with the ball is tackled.

You can widen the channel and play the same exercise with three attackers versus two defenders.

Dummy

In a two v one situation, when the defender doesn't move to tackle the ball-carrier, you may be able to use a dummy pass. The dummy pass is a classic piece of trickery where you fake making a pass, drawing the defender towards the receiver, only for you not to make the pass and continue running. However, no support, no dummy, so make sure you have a team-mate in the position you intend to dummy.

Defender is not committed to tackling the ball-carrier and is drifting across towards the receiver. The ball-carrier swings his arms across his body as if to make the pass. Defender heads more towards the receiver.

Ball-carrier whips ball back into the chest and runs free.

Look to combine a dummy pass with acceleration away and, if you can, a swerve.

Loop

Another excellent way of creating an overlap is via what is called a loop pass. This is when a player passes the ball to a receiver and then runs hard in a loop around to become available for a pass. Done well, it's like playing with an extra man in attack.

Player makes pass...

... then loops around back of team-mates to make another attacker.

The switch pass

Sometimes known as the scissors, the switch pass can be used to change the direction of the ball and can outwit a defence. Successful switch passing starts with the ball-carrier. He must run in a way that threatens the defence, usually starting straight on and then angling his run to head between defender and receiver. The receiver angles his run also, but in a line that crosses with the ball-carrier. The pass is made when the ball-carrier and receiver cross.

As the run is angled, the ball-carrier must shield the ball from the defender. By keeping the ball shielded on the side furthest from the defender, the ball-carrier also shows the ball to the receiver throughout the move.

As players cross, the ball-carrier twists at the waist and lobs a soft pass a little in front of the receiver for the receiver to run on to, collect and move away.

Receiver must cross BEHIND the ball-carrier otherwise he cannot receive a pass *and* is likely to be penalised for obstruction.

Switch square

Mark out a 15m or so square and stand two rows of players
at the corners. The ball-carrier and receiver head off to the
middle of the square, running diagonally. As they cross, the
pass is made and the players head off at an angle, allowing
the next pair of players to run.

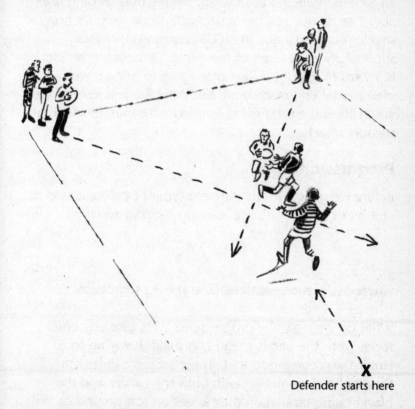

X
Defender starts here

To practise the switches and dummy switches together,
place a defender who moves into the middle at the same
time as the other players. The defender has to guess which
player is going to keep the ball – in other words, if it's a
switch pass or a dummy move – and make a tackle.

5 Tackling

So, so important. Remember all my comments earlier about how size doesn't matter? Well, if that applies anywhere, it applies to tackling. Simply put, tackling is all about technique not brute strength. Done well, it's how smaller backs manage to tackle enormous forwards successfully at all levels of the game. One such example is 1.74m (5'9") David Rees managing to bring down man-mountain Jonah Lomu, but it applies just as much to you halting the progress of your school's muscleman in a friendly match.

Progression

Before we get on to the different types of tackle, let's look at a bit of maths – it's the learning tackling equation.

$$P = MC^2$$

where MC = **m**ore **c**onfidence and P = **p**rogression.

What do we mean by progression? Well, take any one tackle from the pages ahead and build slowly up to it. How? I was coming to that. These tackles can be run through in slow motion with both the tackler and the player being tackled on their knees on soft ground or even indoors on gym-style crash mats. They also give you the opportunity to learn how to fall properly when being tackled. Moving on from there, you, as tackler, can adopt a crouched position and get the player to be tackled to walk through the move. Build the move up from a walk to a slow jog and so on.

Here you can see the side tackle being practised from a kneeling position. It means you have less distance to fall and can concentrate on getting your body position (back flat, shoulder making contact with thigh, arms wrapped around legs) right.

Practising tackling tips

- Loosen up before tackling practice with some physical strengthening exercises such as piggy-back walks and bear-hug lifts.
- For early tackling sessions, wear soft shoes or, if inside, just socks.
- Try to work with someone of your size and weight.

Confidence

Tackling is all about confidence. A player scared of making a tackle is a player who won't make the tackle well and may get hurt. That is why you should work up to tackles if you're nervous.

Being tackled

From whatever angle the tackle comes – front, side or behind – you should be safe from anything worse than the bump from landing on the ground if you follow the basic rules.

As an attacker with the ball you're doing your best to avoid being tackled and should seek to drive through or hand-off weak or poorly timed attempts. However, you quickly learn when you have met your match in a tackle. As soon as you feel arms tighten around your legs or lower body, and you start to fall, two things should be on your mind and in this order: fall safely to the ground and make the ball available to your team-mates.

Fall in the direction of the tackle. Impact with the ground should follow the sequence, knees, thighs and hips and finally, shoulder. Bend your knees, keep tucked up and don't stick out a straight arm to break your fall. Roll from your shoulder to your side to help absorb the force of landing. It's similar to the technique used by parachutists and, if it's good enough for a fall from 1000m, then, surely, it's good enough for you.

Basic tackling rules

When a player with the ball is tackled, he must release the ball immediately, move away from the ball, and get to his feet before playing the ball again. If a ball-carrier falls down but is not held in a tackle, he can get up and continue running forwards. This is why, when tackling a player, you should hold on firmly until the player is fully grounded.

Support player must be on his feet to play the ball.

Tackled player manages to place the ball so that it is available for a team-mate.

Principles of perfect tackling

Most types of tackle work on the same set of basic principles. I'll cut a deal with you – if you read these principles below carefully, I won't repeat them in full for each tackle. Can't say fairer than that, can I?

Up and open

Head up and eyes open. I know it's understandable to get your head down, close your eyes and brace yourself for impact but if you do that, impact may never come. You must always follow the line of your tackle and focus your eyes on your tackle target area – where your shoulder makes contact with the opposition player, which in most cases is the top of the thigh just below the hips.

Thinking ahead

Stay balanced and track the player you intend tackling. Don't aim your tackle for where the player is or was. Aim it for where he will be by the time you make contact – in effect, this means another pace ahead.

No anticipation – no tackle.

Cheeky!

With all tackles, the aim is to stop the attacker with the ball from progressing. You want to make firm contact with your shoulder, quickly getting your arms around the player's lower body or thighs. A general rule with the side, front and rear tackles is to think, "cheek to cheek" – your face cheek should be to the side of one of his bottom cheeks.

Dangerous tackling

NEVER tackle around the head or neck. It's dangerous and causes injury. Yes, attackers can dip down into a tackle, making your handiwork look worse than it is. However, you should never be aiming at the chest or upper back anyway. You want to get low, below the attacker's centre of gravity. Why? Because tackling low is far more likely to unbalance your opponent, causing him or her to fall to the ground which is what you want.

Note to all rugby backs

Make no mistake, good tackling is as valuable an asset in your game as searing pace or a fancy side-step, in fact, more so. You'll get plenty of tackling chances in every rugby match whereas opportunities to show your one-on-one attacking prowess will occur less often.

Something missing...

Thomas Gordon won three caps for Ireland over a hundred years ago, which makes him the only one-handed player to play an international match.

The side tackle

A very common tackle in rugby and one you've already seen part of in the progressions section.

Target area is just below waist level which will be hit with one shoulder. Look to drive off the opposite leg to the shoulder you will be making contact with.

Drive into the tackle using your full body weight making sure that your head slips behind the player being tackled, not in front. This is absolutely vital if you want to avoid injuries.

Wrap your arms around the player's legs and hold on tight. Drive through the player with your legs and turn the ball-carrier sideways as you fall. If you've tackled well, you should land partly on top of him.

Side tackle drill

Once you're comfortable with the side tackle, in the kneeling and walk through phases, try this excellent drill:

Tacklers

This player must attempt to side tackle the player with the ball.

Try line

Both players set off at the same time.

Player with the ball must attempt to reach the try line.

Once a tackle is completed or a try scored, players return to the back of the line and the next pair set off.

Ball-carriers

10m square box

Front tackle

The basic front tackle sees you using the ball-carrier's momentum to bring him down. Drop into a crouch to receive the ball-carrier on one shoulder, keeping your eyes open and focused on your target. Make sure your head is kept to one side of the ball-carrier's body and keep your head up, chin off chest, and your neck firm. From your crouched position, sit and fall backwards as contact is made with the ball-carrier's legs. Wrap your arms around your opponent's legs and grip tightly. Let the momentum of your opponent carry him over your shoulder and twist so that you land on top of his legs, to the right if you used the right shoulder and to the left if you used the left shoulder to make the tackle.

The more-aggressive slam or blockbuster tackle is used a lot in rugby league (see page 114) and occasionally in rugby union for try-stopping tackles where the player with the ball is forced back away from the try line. For the moment, you've got enough tackling on your plate to leave that one until you're stronger and more experienced.

Front tackle drill

Twin rows of ball-carriers and supporting players.

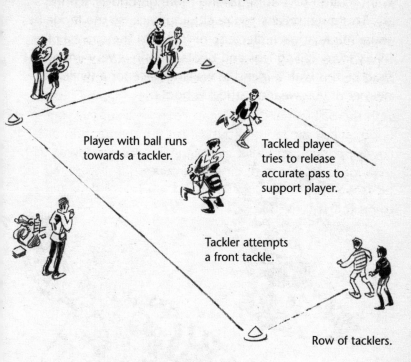

Player with ball runs towards a tackler.

Tackled player tries to release accurate pass to support player.

Tackler attempts a front tackle.

Row of tacklers.

Once tackle is made, players on the ground get up quickly and run to back of their lines. Switch tacklers, ball-carriers and support player rows over after a number of tackles.

Morale-booster

A good tackle anywhere on the pitch can boost your team's morale. A good tackle halts an attacking side's advance and may allow team-mates to regroup and support. If, as a result, your team manages to turn over and get possession of the ball then it's an even better result.

Tackle from behind

Used when the player with the ball is past you and you want to stop him from gaining more ground or scoring a try. This often means you're chasing back, so the tackle has to be made at pace. Because of this, and the chance of injury from flailing legs and boots, timing is very important. Practise this with a friend at walking pace for a while with neither of you wearing studded boots.

Sock practice in the garden.

Match practice with boots on.

The target area is the upper half of the bottom so that your head is to the side of the ball-carrier's behind. You must hit the target area with your shoulder.

Watch the player, time your contact and try to get your back flat, parallel with the ground when you launch into the tackle.

Make contact with your shoulder with your arms encircling the thighs of your opponent. Squeeze tight.

Drive forwards with your shoulder and pull your opponent's legs to one side. Aim to land on top of the player if you can.

Enjoy your tackling

It's five points plus a possible further two from the conversion kick when a try is scored. Effectively, a try-saving tackle in defence is just as important as a try scored at the other end. Take pleasure and pride in good tackling. A tough-tackling side at any level of rugby, and I do mean any level, is a side that is much, much harder to beat.

Smother and tap tackles

Smother tackle

Used mainly in the danger zone near your try line and when you know you are the last or next-to-last line of defence to repel an attack. A smother tackle is more ambitious than a regular tackle because it has not one, but two, objectives: to stop the attacker with the ball from making further progress (like all tackles) and to prevent him from passing to one of his attacking team-mates.

Unlike the rest of the tackles shown so far, the target area for the smother tackle is much higher up the opponent's body. What you are trying to do is to engulf the player's arms so that he cannot release the ball.

STEP 1

Approach the opponent in a more upright stance than for other tackles. The target area is the upper chest and shoulder, which will be hit with one of your shoulders so that your head is to one side of the opponent's.

STEP 2

Accelerate into the tackle, wrapping your arms around your opponent's upper body attempting to trap his arms and the ball. Continue to drive into the tackle.

STEP 3

As both you and your opponent fall to the ground, try to keep the ball smothered. Your momentum should move you so that you land on top of your opponent.

Tripping – no, tapping – yes

In no situation are you allowed to stick out a foot and trip up an opponent. It's against the rules and can be very dangerous. What you can do is tap tackle a fast-moving opponent. A tap tackle is used when an opponent is getting away from you or is out of reach for a full tackle. With outstretched arms you aim to catch one of his ankles or give it a firm tap. This can knock a player off balance, causing him to fall. Yes, he can get back up again, but it may give you or a team-mate time to make a full tackle on him. Remember, a tap tackle is only a last resort when you're not close enough for a full contact tackle.

71

Practical tackling

Good tackling throughout a side is the result of plenty of tackling practice. There are lots of different tackling drills – get your coach to show you a range.

Tackle bags

If your school or club has them, tackling bags are great fun. They're excellent for improving your tackling technique and also for building confidence if you're a little nervous about launching yourself into tackles. Unlike a fellow player, tackling bags don't have stray legs or boots to give you a nasty jolt.

Here's a fun drill using a tackle bag that is useful for both tackling and support play.

A tackle bag with a rugby ball sitting on top. Tackler launches into bag, spilling the ball.

Support player collects ball and runs on.

Player rights tackle bag and places another ball on top for next tackler and support player.

6 Possession and recycling

In attack, you are trying to avoid contact with defenders but it will happen at some point or other. Once contact is made, there may be a number of options from the gut pass to the ruck or maul. Before we get into them, some words on tactics from rugby strategist, Dr Troy Loin.
Over to you, Troy.

Thank you, Clive. What I want to talk to you about here is recycling – not taking cola bottles to the bottle bank or, like the author here, re-using old jokes, but maintaining possession of the rugby ball. In attack, play often goes through a series of phases with the ball-carrier stopped or tackled by the defence. Keeping the ball in your side's hands and recycling it quickly and cleanly through a series of plays is called continuity. If you can keep continuity throughout a series of phases, you have a great chance of scoring points.

Thanks, Troy.

Bump and guts

Once contact is made, it's the job of the ball-carrier and support players to keep possession of the ball and, if possible, to move it away quickly from the contact area. Two methods for this, if you can stay on your feet, are the bump and the gut pass.

The bump pass

This is the easiest and often the first option you will consider when facing immediate contact with an opposition player. As you approach contact, begin to lead with one shoulder. Lower your body towards the ground and push the ball back and away from the contact area. Make sure you've still got two hands firmly on it. Make your last stride a long low one, if possible, and bump up into your opponent's midriff. If you make a good contact, he may be forced back a short distance, giving you the time to make a short pass to a supporting player.

Don't step too far into defender.

Ensure wide base and good stance.

The gut pass

So-called because the ball is finally passed at stomach height. This move is used when you're to the side of the defender.

Make contact as in the bump, but look to roll the contact from your shoulder to your back. You use your front foot as a pivot, allowing you to turn through a quarter of a circle until you can see a team-mate in support. Push or pass the ball into a supporting player's chest region. The support player should lean forwards and get one hand under and one hand over the ball. Once they have the ball, they should stay low and drive forwards, beyond the defender. The first ball-carrier now becomes a supporting player.

Stay on your feet

Both the bump and gut pass rely on you staying on your feet throughout contact. Coaches are constantly going on about players staying on their feet and with good reason. If you're on your feet, you're in the game – if you're on the floor, you're out of it. Simple as that.

Ball retention

Support

Good support is vital for all attempts at retaining the ball after contact. This especially applies to the first support player to arrive. If the ball-carrier is on their feet and looks like they can get a pass away, the support player must shout which side they are coming from. If the ball-carrier is standing, but is held up in a tackle, the support player looks to seal off the ball from the opposition, by closing around the ball-carrier. He should try to get his hands on the ball and drive the ball-carrier forwards.

On the ground

Good tackling will bring you to the ground. When you fall, try to turn so that your body is between the ball and the opposition. Place the ball an arm's length away. This brings the ball closer to your support players and makes it clearer if an opposition player dives over the top – an infringement called killing the ball.

Good ball presentation here. The player's body is at right-angles to the touch line with the ball an arm's length back.

Ball on the ground

With the ball on the ground, the support player has the choice of falling on the ball and trying to bounce back up or lifting the ball up immediately and moving forwards. With lifting, it's essential that you step over the ball to fill the space in front of the ball before you pick it up. Lead with one shoulder and bend your knees and hips to get low as your back foot is planted close to the ball. Keep your eyes on the ball as you collect it and move it to your chest, then accelerate away.

Player steps over the ball.

Player gets low to collect the ball with both hands.

Player moves away with the ball gripped firmly.

Rucks

Right, definition first. A ruck is when the ball is on the ground and one or more players from each team are on their feet and in physical contact, closing around the ball. Rucks occur when a player has been tackled and the ball is grounded. Well-organised rucks can produce quick attacking ball, disorganise an opposition's defence and can allow backs to see when the ball is coming out so that they can time their attacking runs. On the other hand, rucks can make the ball difficult to control and don't tend to work well unless your team is going forwards.

The easiest way to detail what happens in a ruck is to show one, so here is one in action.

The ball-carrier makes contact with his leading shoulder and tries to bump the tackler away. If held or brought to ground, he or she falls slowly (to buy time for supporting players) and turns towards the support as much as possible.

As the ball-carrier hits the ground, he places the ball at arm's length before covering his ears with his hands, elbows up. This provides him with protection as his support players quickly arrive and start to drive in from behind the ball, over the top.

As the support players drive, they look to bind on to either an opposition player or one of their team-mates. The drive position is a low one with head up and forward, eyes open and back flat with shoulders above the hips.

Support players stay on their feet as they drive firmly forwards. They shrug their shoulder on contact and try to keep their opponents on their feet, too. Once the ball-carrier is clear of the ruck, he gets to his feet and prepares to support the next play.

Scrum Half

A good, forwards-moving ruck should release the ball for the scrum half or acting scrum half to pick the ball up and make the next move. However, a forward can decide to pick the ball up and drive around the fringe of the ruck, setting up the next phase of play.

Mauls

Mauls are where one or more players from each team close around a player holding the ball. The ball is not on the floor like in a ruck, but firmly in a player's hands. Mauls tend to be less dynamic than rucks and usually result in slower ball. However, they can be useful in a range of situations.

The ball-carrier partly turns and uses his leading shoulder to hunch up over the ball offering it maximum protection. In comes the first support player who drives just under the ball and upwards, using the opposite shoulder to the ball-carrier.

The ball-carrier steps to the tackler's side to unbalance him, making contact with his leading shoulder. Establish a wide stance with knees bent to stay on your feet. The ball is kept visible to the support player who lays his hands on the ball, one above, one below.

The ball-carrier and support player attempt to drive forwards or, if under pressure, to stay their ground and on their feet until further support arrives. New supporting team-mates can only join a maul from behind the furthest back foot of a player already in the maul. New support binds over the ball-carriers and helps to keep the players on their feet.

There are several options at this point. The maul can keep driving forwards, a player can attempt to roll around the edge of the maul with his team-mates supporting or, as shown here, the ball can be worked to the back of the maul for a pass to the scrum half or acting scrum half.

Options, options

There are a number of options in the maul that you may be able to take, depending on the situation. Relatively early on in the maul, the first support player can take the ball, if he so wishes, and either run with it or pass to another incoming support player. Later on, a rolling maul can be developed. Whatever option is chosen, protection of the ball and communication between team-mates are paramount, as is staying on your feet.

More mauling and a handy drill

Rolling maul

The ball can be uncoupled (team-mates' hands removed) and one player at the back, leading with one shoulder and largely facing towards his team-mates, can roll around the edge of the maul. Team-mates support this new ball-carrier as before, noting the direction of this wheeling movement and maintaining it to create a rolling maul. A rolling maul can be used to get over a try line or to suck in defenders on the fringes of a maul whilst still moving forwards. It can be hard to start, requires great teamwork and is not the fastest move in the world but, if done well, a good rolling maul can eat up a surprisingly large amount of ground and is hard to stop.

Quiz

1. Where is the 2003 World Cup going to be held?
2. Who currently holds the record for the most points scored in a World Cup match?
3. Has 15-a-side rugby ever been an Olympic sport?
4. Which players have the following nicknames; Campo, Merv The Swerve, Pine Tree?

Answers on page 127.

Support and ball presentation drill

Let's finish off this brief chapter with a handy drill all about ball retention and support. It's a tiring but valuable exercise involving a line of four or more tacklers 10m or so apart and two players who switch support and ball-carrying roles down the line.

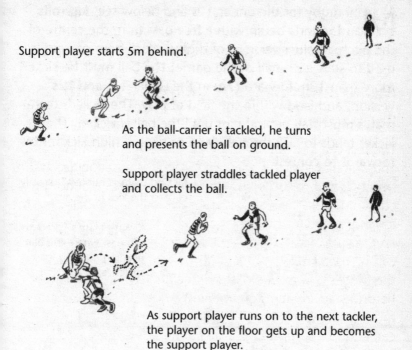

Support player starts 5m behind.

As the ball-carrier is tackled, he turns and presents the ball on ground.

Support player straddles tackled player and collects the ball.

As support player runs on to the next tackler, the player on the floor gets up and becomes the support player.

Work your way down the line then swap roles.

Sorry, but...

That's all we've got room for on ball retention, rucking and mauling. We reckon you are best to follow your coach's instruction on technique and strategy. These sorts of plays are best practised with team-mates in training sessions so that every member of the side knows what is going on.

The kick-off, restarts and set plays

Starts and restarts

Mini rugby for the under 10s and below sees kick-offs and restarts begin with a free pass from the centre of the pitch. In older versions of rugby, a kick from ground is used to start each half of the game. The ball must be kicked more than 10m forward (7m in the under 11s and 12s version) and land within the field of play. The kicker's team-mates must stay behind him until the ball is kicked. The kicker tends to kick the ball deep or hang a high kick for his forwards to contest.

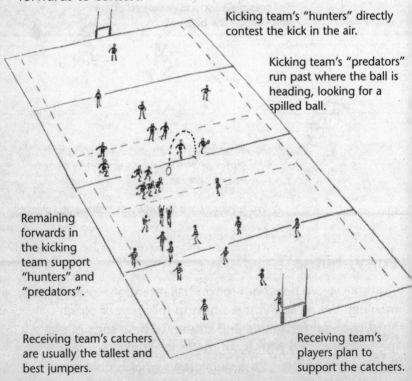

Kicking team's "hunters" directly contest the kick in the air.

Kicking team's "predators" run past where the ball is heading, looking for a spilled ball.

Remaining forwards in the kicking team support "hunters" and "predators".

Receiving team's catchers are usually the tallest and best jumpers.

Receiving team's players plan to support the catchers.

Halfway line drop-outs

After a try has been scored and a conversion has been successful, play is restarted from the halfway line but, unlike the kick-off, the ball is drop kicked into play. All the above strategies and techniques usually apply.

22m drop-outs

These occur when the ball is propelled into the defending team's in-goal area by the attacking side but is grounded by the defending team. Examples include a long punt and a failed conversion or penalty kick. Play is resumed by the kicker kicking the ball from anywhere along, and either on or behind, his team's 22m line. As this picture shows, the kicker has a number of options.

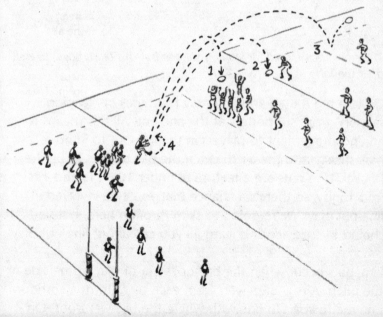

1. Ball up for forwards to contest in the air.
2. Ball up and behind the opposition's forwards for team-mates to chase.
3. Ball kicked long so that the opposition has to attack from deep.
4. Short kick to himself to set up a surprise running play.

Line-outs

The crowd has roared for leaping salmon but this team have taken it a bit too far!

Go to a big match and you may hear cries of "leaping salmon" from supporters at the line-out. All this means is an encouragement to players in the line-out to jump majestically into the air to catch the ball thrown in by the hooker. Line-outs are a feature of under 10s, 11s and 12s mini rugby, so there's a chance that you'll be involved in line-out play. We're going to skim through here, but you should seek advice and learn all you can about line-out play.

Line-outs occur when the ball goes out of play at the side of the pitch. A row of players from each team form a corridor one metre apart in line with where the ball went out. On the opposite page, we've shown a line-out from a full game with seven players in the line. In mini rugby, line-outs are restricted to two, three or four players.

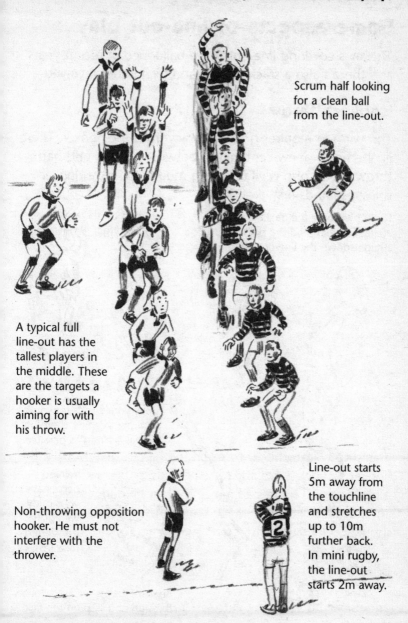

Scrum half looking for a clean ball from the line-out.

A typical full line-out has the tallest players in the middle. These are the targets a hooker is usually aiming for with his throw.

Non-throwing opposition hooker. He must not interfere with the thrower.

Line-out starts 5m away from the touchline and stretches up to 10m further back. In mini rugby, the line-out starts 2m away.

The hooker's throw must be straight down the middle, otherwise the referee will award a new line-out with the other team given the throw-in.

Some aspects of line-out play

The laws covering line-outs have ballooned in recent years and there's also a stack of skills and techniques involved.

Hooker's throw

Throwing in requires great accuracy from the hooker. There is often only a few centimetres between a good and bad throw. Good grip is vital so, in a muddy game, a hooker dries his hands first.

Ball is held near the back with hands along the seam and the point facing straight down the line-out.

Focus on the area above your target jumper.

Move your hands forwards to throw, keeping them on the ball as long as possible.

Release occurs as your body weight is transferred forwards.

After the ball is released, follow through and step on the field.

If you're a budding hooker, you can practise your throw on your own with a target area chalked high up on a wall and you standing the correct distance back.

The catcher's options

If the ball comes cleanly to a line-out player, he has two options. He can pat the ball with his inside arm only, back to the scrum half who can immediately pass it out to launch an attack. Otherwise he can get both hands on the ball, bring it in to his body and set up some form of driving play from the line-out.

Line-out player uses his inside arm.

Scrum half receives the ball.

Variations on a theme

All experienced teams have their own line-out variations. Two of the most basic are the short and long throws. In both cases, the hooker shapes to throw to the usual middle of the line but actually throws either directly to the front player or right to the back. Each variation has its own merits. When you've been struggling in the middle of your line and are near your own try line, a short throw, followed by your forwards grouping round can be a safe play. When attacking, and gifted with some fabulous backs, a riskier long throw to the back of the line can release a potent attack. It all depends on the situation.

The scrummage

Despite great changes to the rugby laws, the scrummage, or scrum as it's usually shortened to, is still a vital part of the game. Cries of "Heave!" echo around all rugby grounds whenever a scrum is called.

Scrums are given for a number of reasons, particularly when an attack fails due to an infringement and the opposition is unable to take advantage. Once a scrummage is signalled by a referee, a set number of forwards from each side link together to form a scrummage. In under 12s and under 11s rugby, five-man scrummages are used and in under 10s and below, just three players per side form a scrummage. In the full game, eight players a side are used.

Safe scrummaging

Unlike many of rugby's skills, scrummages should only be practised under the eye of an experienced coach. They can be extremely dangerous unless everyone knows what to do. Whatever your place in the scrummage, you should adopt a safe scrummaging position as shown here.

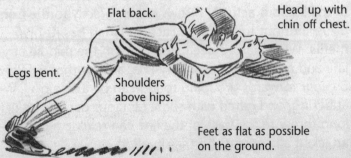

Flat back.

Head up with chin off chest.

Legs bent.

Shoulders above hips.

Feet as flat as possible on the ground.

It's binding

Players link in a specific way, called binding, before
engaging the opposition players in the scrummage. Each
position calls for a particular method of binding that should
allow all players to adopt the safe scrummaging position.
You have to stay in the scrum until the ball is out.

Front row binding.

*How the two locks bind
together.*

How locks fit into front row.

*How flankers bind to locks in
the eight-man scrum.*

All bindings should be strong and tight.

Locking horns

The order of movement into the scrum can be summed up in four words: crouch, touch, pause and engage. The two sets of forwards engage only once the referee gives the signal to do so. The front row is not for the squeamish so candidates should be strong, ideally short-necked and broad-shouldered, and not mind a bit of physical contact. Ex-England rugby captain, Bill Beaumont, who always played as a lock, was once asked by the then England manager, Alec Lewis, after a front row team-mate had been sent off, "Have you ever played prop forward or will the next 75 minutes be your first time?" Bill fortunately survived, but this never happens today. Only players with experience in the front row play there and international replacements always include specialist front-row players.

Winning by a neck

"The more muscles you can develop in the neck and shoulders, the less chance of injury." Not my words but those of Jason Leonard, one of the great England props. One simple neck-strengthener is trying to pull and push your neck in different directions as a friend holds you and resists your moves. Don't jerk or roll your head – just firmly, continuously push.

The put-in and hooking

There's a stack of rules connected with the ball's entry into the scrum and what happens to it afterwards. Basically the scrum half has to put the ball straight into the tunnel – the area of space between the opposing front rows. As the ball hits the ground in the tunnel, the hooker looks to hook the ball back through his side of the scrum where it will usually come under the control of the team's no.8. As the put-in occurs, both teams will attempt to drive back with their thighs to gain distance.

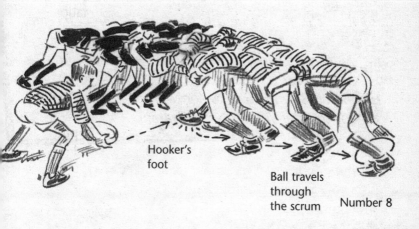

Hooker's foot

Ball travels through the scrum

Number 8

The put-in is all about timing between the scrum half and the hooker. The opposition half of the scrum will seek to get a big shove on to disrupt the ball and drive back the team with the ball. Occasionally, the opposition hooker will attempt to win the ball for his team – known as "a scrum against the head". In reality, it is increasingly rare to see teams achieve this, but that shouldn't stop you from trying!

Collapsing scrum

Both packs at a scrum are trying to maintain the stability of the scrum, or at least their half of it. Sometimes, though, the forces involved are unequal and the scrums turn, known as wheeling round. If a scrum wheels round more than 90°, the referee will call for a new scrummage. Occasionally, a scrum collapses. If you feel a scrum collapsing, drop to your knees before your head hits the ground. Release your arms to absorb the weight on your elbows and forearm.

Technique over strength

Scrummaging requires tremendous concentration and resolve. It can be enormously strength-sapping especially against bigger and stronger opponents. But technique has an incredibly important part to play. A forward pack with great technique can overcome a heavier, supposedly stronger opposition with poorer technique. It happens more often than you think.

Quiz

1. Two famous English clubs wear letters instead of numbers on their shirts. Can you name them?
2. Which rugby playing country's symbol on their jerseys is a silver fern?
3. Which famous English club side plays at the Recreation Ground?

Answers on page 127.

Attacking options

Assuming the ball has been hooked well and is at the back of the scrum, your team have a number of options. Many times your team's scrum half will pick the ball up from the base of the scrum and pass to the fly half who decides to either kick upfield, kick for touch, pass or run with the ball himself. The scrum half may choose not to pass outside and, instead, to kick or run with the ball himself.

This scrum half has picked up the ball and made a run down the blind side of the scrum catching the opposition unawares.

Diving pass

Here's one of the passes a scrum half can use at the base of a scrum or a ruck. The player dives in the direction of the pass, releasing the ball when he is most stretched out.

Head up with eyes on the receiver.

Hands pointing towards the target.

Now, what we've shown above is just the start of good scrummaging and line-out technique. It's an area where there is no substitute for hands-on coaching.

8 Kick it!

Kicking creeps into mini rugby once you start playing under 11s and under 12s. In these games, as in the full game, kicking isn't just for scrum and fly halves and place kickers. There are many kicks that can be used to great effect by all players in a team. Two things to note: with the exception of goal-kicking, practise kicking with both feet and, in a match, kick only when necessary. There's a big chance you won't recover possession so you must have a good reason for kicking, either a safety-first option (such as kicking to touch from your own 22m area) or the chance of an attacking breakthrough (the grubber kick, below).

Grubbers

A grubber is a low kick along the ground with the ball travelling end over end. It can be used effectively in attack to get the ball behind opposition defenders deep in the opponent's half. It's particularly effective when you are aware of a team-mate sprinting through unmarked to the try line. It's also useful in defence when you have no support, want to put the ball in touch but are out of your 22 so cannot kick the ball out on the full.

Everybody off!

A violent match in 1982 between Didcot and Abingdon saw the referee Peter Richards send off all 30 players. "They didn't seem to be too interested in wanting to play rugby," was his understated comment.

Hold the ball vertically with one hand on each side. Keep your head over the ball with your eyes on it. Lean forwards in a balanced position and release the ball.

Bring your kicking foot through to make contact just before the ball reaches the ground.

Punch the ball along the ground keeping your leg low and straight.

Foot should be pointing down and contact made by your laces hitting the upper half of the ball.

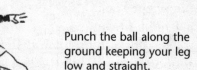

The amount of force you put into contact with the ball and how far it travels forwards is known as the weight of a kick and is especially important with grubber kicks over the try line for a team-mate to chase. Practise grubber kicks aiming to reach reasonably large targets (to allow for the oval ball's wanderings) 10m, 15m and 20m away.

97

Punting

Three reasons why you may want to use this aerial kick:

1 to clear the ball as far upfield as possible.
2 to find touch when the ball is in hand.
3 because you've taken a mark and have to kick the ball! (see page 45).

"No, Charlie, not that sort of punting!"

Rear hand same side as your kicking foot. Forward hand halfway down the ball, fingers pointing along the seams.

Contact made with the top face of your boot on the laces.

Select target then keep your eyes on the ball which is held at waist height in both hands. The ball should be pointing slightly down and away from your kicking side. Your non-kicking leg holds your body weight. Stay balanced.

The ball should not be thrown up into the air but just dropped down. It's quicker and helps to keep the ball at the right angle for contact with your boot. Swing your leg and make firm contact with the ball.

Your leg naturally accelerates through the kick, like a golf club swinging through the ball. Finish with a good high follow-through with your kicking leg straight and your body leant slightly forwards. Greater height and distance come from timing and a smooth action not brute force.

Foot should be pointed at the moment of impact.
Arm on your non-kicking side swings through.

Up and under

Also known as the high punt or garryowen, this attacking kick is used to get the ball behind the three-quarter line and not too close to the opposition full-back or wings. The technique is very similar to a punt except that the ball is hit for height and usually for less distance.

Ball starts pointed directly away from you. It's dropped vertically and kicked in the centre. Aim for your boot laces to be the first and main point of impact. A high follow-through afterwards is important.

Drop kicks

A kick between the posts during open play is worth a whopping three points so all players, backs especially, should be aware of the opportunity and practise drop kicks. It is also the kick used for drop-outs on your 22m line and for re-starts after points have been scored. The ball is kicked on the half volley, which is as it touches the ground.

Ball held vertically, hands on either side. This is your last look at the target. From now on, your eyes should remain on the ball.

As the ball is released, straight down so that it remains vertical, your kicking foot starts its swing. Keep your head down and your weight on your non-kicking foot.

Contact is made a third of the way up just as the ball reaches the ground. Your kicking foot swings through and lifts the ball into the air. Follow through the ball with a high action.

Drop kick practice

Drop kicks can be practised with one or more friends. Set a marker down 20–25m either side of the posts. One player takes a drop kick from this distance. The player on the other side of the posts attempts to catch the ball cleanly or collect it after its bounces. This player runs back to the marker and makes a drop kick back to the first player.

Here's one variation that requires two more mates.

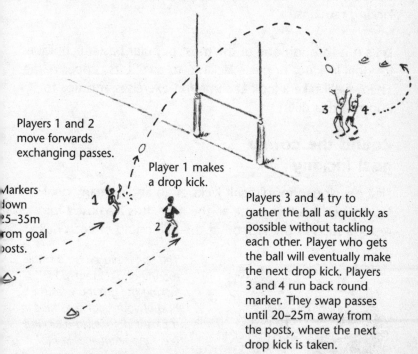

Players 1 and 2 move forwards exchanging passes.

Player 1 makes a drop kick.

Markers down 25–35m from goal posts.

Players 3 and 4 try to gather the ball as quickly as possible without tackling each other. Player who gets the ball will eventually make the next drop kick. Players 3 and 4 run back round marker. They swap passes until 20–25m away from the posts, where the next drop kick is taken.

One of the most famous drop kicks ever was hoisted by Jeremy Guscott for the British Lions against South Africa. With time running out, and with the Lions needing a score, Guscott received the ball and, cool as a cucumber, slotted the ball over for three points and a famous victory.

Kicking for goal

With penalty kicks worth three points and conversions two, you don't have to be a mathematical genius to work out that points awarded for kicks can quickly mount up into a formidable total. In fact, with increasingly good defences and more and more penalties given, many matches are won without a single try being scored. This is a problem that the law-making authorities of rugby are looking to sort out but, in the meantime, the importance of accurate goal kicking remains.

Let's run through one of the most popular basic techniques for goal kicking, or place kicking, to give it its proper name. Then, we'll take a look at some fun exercises and tips to improve this skill.

Round the corner goal kicking

First developed for difficult kicks at an angle, many goal kickers use this technique all the time. It is also used for restarts such as the kick off at the beginning of each half.

The ball is placed on a small mound of dirt created by kicking the ground with the heel of your boot or is held in a plastic disc called a kicking tee. One seam should be facing the kicker.

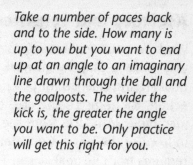

Take a number of paces back and to the side. How many is up to you but you want to end up at an angle to an imaginary line drawn through the ball and the goalposts. The wider the kick is, the greater the angle you want to be. Only practice will get this right for you.

line through ball to middle of posts

angle of run

Your approach to the ball should be steady with your head down and eye on the ball. Get your non-kicking foot planted to the side of the ball and fractionally behind it. This is vital as your body weight should be on this leg.

Swing your leg powerfully but under control right through. Make contact with the instep of your boot about a-third of the way up the ball. Follow through in front and slightly across your body.

Accuracy and consistency

Work on your goal kicking as much as you can, and when you've done that much, work some more. The secret of goal kicking is all about practice to groove your kicking action. It's no use being able occasionally to thump over incredible 35m kicks from the sideline when you miss sitters in front of the posts. Consistent accuracy is what a team requires from its goal kicker. This stems from you getting into a routine and repeating it so that it almost becomes automatic. When practising, always make a number of kicks from the same position and try to feel and note the movements of your body throughout the kick.

Goal kicking practice

Unlike Lord Posh above, you may not have your own rugby pitch, nor may there be one free in the park when you want to practise. Use your imagination and head over to a spare soccer goal. Now, a soccer crossbar is half a metre or so lower and 1.5m wider than the crossbar on rugby posts so you'll have to judge whether the ball really got through the posts. Practise your goal-kicking, ideally with a number of balls and a friend who can retrieve your kicks. Swap after a number of attempts. You can't have all the fun!

Goal kicking guide

- Make sure your steps back and to the side are the same each time.
- During practice, check that your non-kicking foot lands in the same place every time.
- Keep your eye on the ball right through the kick. Don't let your head come up too soon.
- Don't fall away through the kick – losing balance can cause the kick to wander wide.
- Make sure contact is clean and where you want it, near the base of the ball with the lower instep of your boot.

Robot rugby

Did you know that at the 1998 Scottish Rugby Union Cup Final, the kicking tee was ferried on the field by a small remote-controlled truck. What will they think of next?

"He's our substitute goalkicker, Ref — he's extremely accurate!"

9 Scoring tries... and stopping them

Here are some ultra-brief ideas and tips for both bagging tries and stopping them from being scored.

Some very good news...

If you master the basic skills of running, passing, support and good set-piece play, then you're well on the way to good, attacking rugby and attacking rugby leads to tries. Your coach is likely to have a number of set moves and plays he favours for matches. Our advice: listen to him. He's in charge of coaching you and will know your strengths and weaknesses as individual players, and as a team, far better than you will.

Backs work on lots of plays and moves involving loop passes, switches and varying their running lines of attack. Here's one of the moves sometimes employed.

Dummy switch

A variation on the switch pass all the way back in chapter 4, this looks like a switch and ends with the defender committed to tackling the receiver but with the original ball-carrier free to move away, still with the ball. It's quite an advanced move and usually a last-minute decision from the ball-carrier who senses that the defender is reading the switch move and is favouring tackling the receiver.

Defender changes direction to intercept 'new' ball carrier

Rats!

The move starts in the same way as a switch with the players angling their running lines to cross. It's vital that, as the players get close to crossing, the ball is hidden from the defender. Make the movement for a soft pass but quickly withdraw your arms, take the ball into your chest and move away.

Ten (attacking) commandments

I'm sure by now you've had quite enough reading and are itching to get out to the pitch or park to try out some of the moves and skills we've shown you. That's why we've summarised some of the key elements of attacking theory to provide you with these 10 commandments of attacking.

1 Exploit overlaps by making sure that you draw a tackler before passing or by making a dummy pass and breaking through yourself.

2 Communicate with team-mates throughout an attack (and for that matter, in defence). Remember, you're all in the game together.

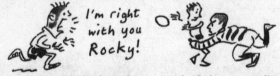

3 Try not to get isolated in attack if there are lines of defence still to get through.

4 If your team wants to use set moves in attack, make sure they are worked on thoroughly in training.

5 Move the ball at speed and with accuracy.

6 Practise quick, clean rucks in training. They can be a key to successful attacks.

7 Remember that if you keep the ball through a number of phases of attacking play, you are more likely to score.

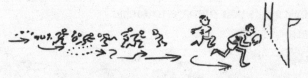

8 Always, always, always support the ball-carrier.

9 When running with the ball, look to head forwards and into space.

10 Only kick as a last resort. It's better to wait for support by creating a maul.

Team defence

Now, your coach will have his or her own ideas regarding exactly how you should be positioned. Yet, there are some general principles of team defence that apply in all situations. Your whole team's defence must be organised with everyone knowing what they're doing and where they should be. Try to go forwards in defence and treat your 22m line like the last line that matters, your try line. This defence is forcing the attacking team wide, but the attack has an extra man over. This potentially dangerous position can be eased by an aware full-back coming up into the defensive line to tackle the extra man when he receives the ball. Quick movement is essential but as you and your team-mates arrive in tackling positions, make sure you are balanced as you prepare to tackle.

Extra player collects ball here

Full-back across to tackle extra attacker

Defenders should look to attack the ball-carrier and close down his support. By cutting out space and options for the opposing team to attack in, a defending team can really pressurise the attack, possibly forcing them into making errors.

Covering back

If the ball is kicked behind your line, get back as quickly as you can between the ball and your try line. This covering back is vital, especially in the last quarter of a game when tiredness starts to become more and more of a factor. The more a team can cover back, the harder it becomes for an attacking side to score a try.

Drift defence

Sometimes the backs in defence look to move or "drift" to the touchline in covering an attack. This drift defence works well when an attack has headed out wide too early or has passed quickly to the winger. But don't just drift out on your own without team-mates adopting the same tactic, otherwise you may leave a try-scoring hole in the defence for an attacker to head through.

Rugby sevens

Want to see lots of attack and defence in action?
Then check out rugby sevens. For non-stop effort and
excitement, it's the bee's knees. Seven players engage in an
all-action 14-minute game (20 minutes in some finals) with
every effort made by the referee to keep the ball in play.
The name of the game with rugby sevens is tries and
both teams are constantly on the look out for incredible
attacking moves, sleight of hand dummies and long passes
to open up the game. It's as exciting and entertaining as
rugby gets and knowing that seven players from each side
play on a FULL-SIZE RUGBY PITCH makes me shudder.

Many junior coaches like to get their players playing sevens,
usually on smaller pitches, whenever possible. It certainly
helps develop your ball-handling and decision-making skills
in attack and your vision of the game and repeated tackling
skills in defence. For both attack and defence, sevens can
really work at your fitness, speed and stamina. In short, it's
hard work but fabulous fun.

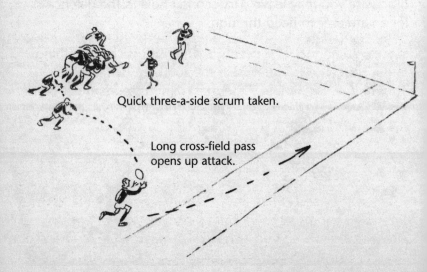

Quick three-a-side scrum taken.

Long cross-field pass
opens up attack.

Conversion kicks after tries must be drop kicks. This keeps the game moving along. A delayed kick can result in the referee disallowing it.

Although national teams from Britain have had some success at international events, sevens isn't such a big thing in the UK as it is in Asia and in the southern hemisphere. The Hong Kong Sevens is the most famous tournament of them all – an incredible spectacle with teams from all over the world competing.

1998 saw rugby sevens introduced into the Commonwealth Games. It was a huge success with some truly brilliant matches including a tense, tough final between New Zealand and Fiji. The Kiwis won 21–14.

113

Rugby league

A different code

Rugby league isn't a version of rugby union, it is a quite separate game with different people in charge, different laws and tactics. It's a fabulous and very dynamic game that has had a number of its innovations adopted by rugby union including:

- Replacements
- Sin bin (in the adult game where a player performing illegal play is sent off the pitch for a period of the game)
- Total rugby – every player being able to tackle and attack
- Dedicated fitness programmes

Here, we've included a few pointers to watching and playing rugby league.

The game – in brief

Rugby league relies on tries (worth four points), conversion kicks after a try (worth two points), penalty kicks (two points again) and drop goals (worth a measly, but sometimes decisive one point). As in union, the ball can be run with, kicked and passed sideways or backwards to a team-mate in order to keep possession. A key difference in the game is the tackling procedure. When a player with the ball is tackled, he stops and plays the ball to a team-mate close behind him. A team is allowed to be tackled five times in a row before a sixth tackle sees possession of the ball pass to the opposition team.

Scrums but no line-outs

There are no line-outs in rugby league. If the ball goes over a touchline in normal play, play is restarted with a scrum 10m in from the touchline at the place where the ball went out of play. Scrums are also awarded for a number of other infringements such as passing forwards and knock-ons. Rugby league's six-man scrum is all about releasing quick ball to the scrum half or loose forward who is positioned at the back of the scrum.

3 front-row players.

1 loose forward at the back of the scrum.

2 second row.

Markings

Pitches are similar to rugby union pitches but with a couple of different sets of markings. There are lines across the width of the pitch marking every 10m, and a pair of lines running the length of the pitch 10m in from the touchline, which are used for tap penalties and scrums.

Running and being tackled

Hard running

Every player on a 13-a-side team is expected to run hard in attack and tackle even harder in defence. The ball must be well protected from the impact of a tackle. The ball is carried either with both hands or with one hand keeping the ball firmly to the chest.

Ball on chest.
Never tuck it
under your arm.

Holding one-handed, leaves your arm free for hand-offs and for generating extra pace.

Tackled!

The player with the ball can be tackled by any number of opposition players. A player is said to be tackled when:

1 He is held by his opponent and the ball, his hand or his arm that holds the ball touches the ground.
2 When he is held up by one or more opponents and cannot make any further progress.
3 When he is held by an opponent and makes it clear that a tackle has been made and he wishes to be released to play the ball.

Playing the ball

Once tackled, a player must get to his feet and play the ball. This means placing the ball on the ground and rolling it backwards with a foot to a team-mate who can then pick up and play the ball.

Player keeps control of the ball in the tackle. Once the tackle has been made, the player gets quickly to his feet.

Defender is allowed to mark the player playing the ball. Other defenders must retreat 5m.

Receiver crouches low, hands outstretched to receive the ball.

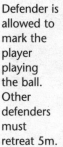

Use the ball of your foot on top of the ball and don't force it back too hard.

Ball-playing tips

Playing the ball quickly means attacks can be sustained and defences have trouble getting back and regrouping. Team-mates need to be in support. If not, an opposition player can dive on the ball after it has been played and gain possession for his side.

Tackling...tackling

Tackle types

Side, back and smother tackles, just like the ones in rugby union are often used. Stay in the tackle until the player is fully grounded or the referee has called a tackle. Once you've tackled a player, you have to get up and off him quickly so that he can play the ball. The referee will penalise you if you take too long, an offence called holding in the tackle.

Blockbuster tackle

Front tackles are used more frequently in rugby league than in union. The passive front tackle (found on page 66) is often used, as is the more spectacular crash or blockbuster tackle.

Drive powerfully towards the target area, your opponent's waist. Your shoulder should make contact with the target area with your head to one side. Arms encircle the tackled player just below the buttocks. Use your legs to drive forwards and upwards and pull and lift with your arms. You should finish on top of the tackled player. Do not try this tackle until you have been taught it properly. It can be dangerous.

Dangerous tackles

Any tackle that might cause injury is outlawed in rugby
league and the tackler penalised. Knees cannot be used in a
tackle. High tackles around the neck or head and spear
tackles, where a player is lifted up and then dropped on his
head, are particularly dangerous and may see the tackler
sent to the sin bin.

Driving through tackles

As in rugby union, a
player looks to evade
tackles and, with one
looming, he can pass
to a team-mate. But
rugby league doesn't
have rucks and mauls
so if a player stays on
his feet he can try to
keep driving forwards
through a tackle to
gain valuable extra
ground.

Tackling and driving through tackles is a vital part of
rugby league and should be practised with tackle bags
and real-life players under a coach's watchful eye.

Touch tackle and play on

A change from tackling practice is to remove tackling from
a small-sided game (six or seven-a-side) on half a pitch.
The tackle is replaced with a two-handed touch by one
player. Once caught in this way, the player with the ball
must play on as usual.

Attack and defence

The defensive line

A defending team does its best to keep a straight line across the width of the pitch standing opposite a player from the other side. Often, the full-back and another support player will hang back ready for the punt kick. The defenders nearest each sideline should stand a little outside (i.e. closer to the sideline than the opposition player they are opposite). Defending teams look to move up in a line together so that no gaps are left and so that players can defend together, often with two tackling an attacker at the same time.

Attacking options

Quick ball from tackles, strong running and quality support from team-mates are all the hallmarks of a good, attacking rugby league side. All the skills of the running game – swerves, sidesteps, hand-offs and driving through tackles – are vital, as is swift, clean passing. Now, you cannot release a pass unless there's someone ready to receive it. This makes support the absolute key. The player with the ball may head off deep into the opposition line. Team-mates must be with him, ready for a pass if a tackle is threatening.

Sixth tackle tactics

The excitement and tension always mounts as a team gets close to the sixth tackle. For the first few tackles in a set of six, an attacking team looks to gain as much territory as possible. If they're in their own half or just inside the opposition's after four or five tackles, a long punt kick is usually made with the hope that chasing team-mates will tackle the opposition deep in their own half. But when closer to the try line, after four or five tackles, an attacking team may try something different – a little chip and chase kick or a sweeping passing move.

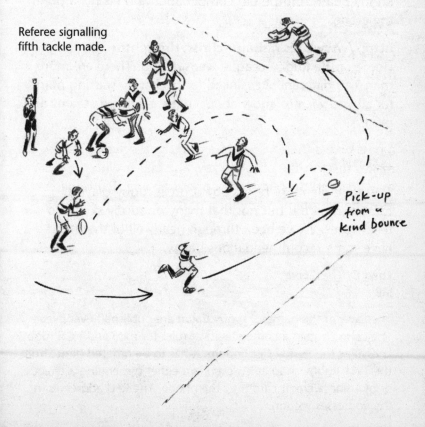

Referee signalling fifth tackle made.

Pick-up from a kind bounce

Want to know more?

Rugby on the Internet

http://www.rfu.com/
Home page of the Rugby Football Union and the first place you should head to on the Net if you're after details of English clubs or players.

http://www.irfb.org/a1.htm
The big cheese of rugby organisation, the International Rugby Board run the big competitions and events around the globe.

http://www2.eis.net.au/~chrisc/rlring.htm
Home of the Rugby League website ring. There are more than 140 different sites linked to this handy starting point for all you wish to know about rugby league, its teams and players.

Books

There are plenty of books about great rugby players, tours and games but not that many on rugby skills and techniques. We've been through nearly all of them and have some recommendations below.

Laws Of The Game
IRB

The Laws of the game of rugby union are published every year. They also contain a complete list of rules for mini and midi rugby, known as the Rugby Continuum. It has to be ordered direct from the TW1 Rugby shop at Twickenham either by sending a cheque or by using a credit card over the phone. The RFU address is in the addresses section.

Rugby: a Player's Guide to the Laws
Derek Robinson
Collins Willow

Although written for adults, this informative and funny
companion guide to the laws is a must if you're serious
about your rugby. Approved by the Rugby Football Union,
the paperback version is pretty cheap, as well.

Heading for the Top
Kerry Wedd
Quiller Press

An excellent book worth hunting out in a good bookshop. It's full
of good training tips and plenty on the techniques needed for
successful attack and defence.

The Handbook of Rugby
Keith Miles
Pelham Books

This book isn't cheap, but it's an excellent volume with more than
200 pages packed full of technique and added tips from some of
the greats of the game.

Rugby Union
Peter Johnson
Crowood Sports Guides

Impressively detailed and well-illustrated book on all the skills
involved in playing rugby union. Good photos, too.

Play the Game: Rugby League
John Huxley
Ward Lock Books

A good starter guide to the rules and some of the skills needed
to play rugby league.

Want to know more?

Rugby magazines

Open Rugby
For rugby league fans, *Open Rugby* is a great read.

Rugby World
Focuses on rugby clubs and sides in Britain and overseas.

Addresses

Rugby Football Union
Twickenham
Middlesex
England
TW1 1DZ
Tel: 020 8892 2000

Welsh Rugby Football Union
Ground Floor
Hidge House
St. Mary Street
Cardiff
Wales
CF1 1DY
Tel: 029 2078 1722

Irish Rugby Football Union
62 Lansdowne Road
Dublin 4
Republic of Ireland
Tel: 1 668 4601

Australian Rugby Football Union
PO Box 188
North Sydney 2060
Australia
Tel: 2 9955 3466

South African Rugby Football Union
PO Box 99
Newlands
7725 South Africa
Tel: 21 685 3038

New Zealand Rugby Football Union
Huddart Parker Building
Post Office Square
PO Box 2172
Wellington
New Zealand
Tel: 4 499 4995

The Rugby Football League
Redhall Lane
Leeds
LS17 8NB
Tel: 0113 2329111

Glossary

Advantage when there is an infringement and the non-offending team takes the opportunity either to score or develop play to gain territory or a better tactical position.

Alignment the shape of the line of backs as they prepare to receive the ball.

Binding a player holding his team-mate's body using his whole arm. It is used in a scrum, a maul and a ruck.

Blind side the narrower side of the pitch between the touch-line and a scrum. (This used to mean the side furthest from the referee.)

Box kick a punt, usually by the scrum half or fly half, that flies over a scrum or line-out for team-mates to chase.

Breakdown the moment when a passage of play, such as passing or running in attack, stops.

Charge down blocking an opponent's kick with the hands, arms or body.

Continuity maintaining possession of the ball through-out a series of phases of play.

Dead ball when the referee blows the whistle to indicate a stoppage of play or when an attempt to convert a try is unsuccessful.

Drift defence a type of defence where defenders gradually move from their opponent immediately opposite to the next player further outside. It only works if the attack heads out wide too early or passes too quickly.

Drive to bind together as a group of players and push the opposition back.

Dummy pass faking to make a pass, going right through the passing movement but retaining the ball and, hopefully, sending the defender the wrong way.

Fair catch if a player inside his own 22 takes the ball cleanly from an opponent's kick, knock-on or throw forwards, he can claim a fair catch by calling, "Mark!" He is then awarded a free kick.

First 5/8th southern hemisphere name for the fly half.

Fixing drawing a defender to one spot in preparation for their tackle, only for the ball-carrier to release a pass to a team-mate that the defender cannot stop.

Foul play any action by a player that is against the spirit and rules of the game including misconduct, dangerous play and obstruction.

Free kick awarded for a fair catch and for a number of offences.

Glossary

Gain line an imaginary line across the pitch through the centre of a scrum, line-out, ruck or maul. If the attacking side crosses this line, then it is gaining ground and moving forwards.

Half backs term for both the fly half and scrum half.

Hand-off using an open palm, a player with the ball may push a tackling player away from him. Hand-offs are outlawed in mini and midi rugby.

Knock-on when the ball touches the hand or arm of a player and moves forwards and touches the ground as a result.

Loop a move involving a player who has just made a pass running around the ball-carrier to his outside so that he becomes available for a return pass.

Midfield players a term for the fly half and the two centres in a team.

Miss pass a pass to a receiver on the ball-carrier's outside which misses out a potential receiver closer to the ball-carrier.

Offside in general play, when a player is in front of the ball after it has last been played off a team-mate. In a scrum, ruck or maul, it is when a player remains or advances in front of the feet that are furthest back. In a line-out, it is when a

player advances within 10m of the middle of the line-out before it has ended.

Open side the area bounded by the scrum and the touchline furthest away from the scrum.

Outside players term for the full-back and wings.

Overlap an attacking sequence that results in attackers outnumbering the defenders and leads to an attack going around the defence.

Peel collecting the ball from the back of a line-out and driving around the end into midfield.

Penalty try a try awarded by a referee when, in the referee's opinion, a player was fouled or obstructed when a try would have resulted. A conversion kick from a try is taken in front of the posts.

Platform the launching point for an attack is usually provided by the forwards at the scrum, line-out, ruck or maul. A good platform is one that is solid and moving forwards.

Pop pass a short, soft pass using almost no hand movement and just some movement of the hands and wrists.

Possession having the ball under control.

Put-in when the scrum half puts the ball into the scrummage.

Recycle maintaining and using possession after making contact with the opposition.

Replacement rugby's term for a substitute player.

Glossary

Rip the action of aggressively wrestling the ball away from an opponent.

Second 5/8th the southern hemisphere name for the inside centre, usually numbered 12.

Sidestep a sudden change of forward direction used by the ball-carrier to get past a defender.

Smother tackle a tackle that cloaks the upper body preventing the ball-carrier getting a pass away.

Spilled ball when a ball-carrier gets tackled hard and loses control of the ball.

Stand-off half or stand-off another name for the fly half.

Strike runner a player who intends breaking through the defence.

Tackle line an imaginary line where contact between the two teams takes place.

Tap kick a tiny kick by a player to himself from a restart situation. The tap kick then allows the player to pass or run with the ball.

Tap tackle a firm tap of the opponent's ankles by a defender's hand causing the tackled player to trip and fall. Also known as an ankle tap.

Touch rugby a non-contact form of the game where a two-handed touch replaces a tackle.

Upfield the area furthest away from your own goal line.

Up and under another term for the garryowen or high, hanging kick.

Answers to Quiz questions

page 82
1. Australia
2. New Zealand (145 v Japan in 1995)
3. Yes (1900–1924)
4. David Campese, Mervyn Davies, Colin Meads

page 94
1. Leicester and Bristol
2. New Zealand
3. Bath

Index